ISBN:978-1-9162807-0-0

Photographs by Michael Nathan-Pepple

Layout and Printing by www.beamreachuk.co.uk

All About

Antigua and Barbuda

Discover the history and heritage of this twin island nation, through some of its top sites and attractions

by

Michael Nathan-Pepple

KEY

St. John
1. Sir Vere Cornwall Bird Sr
2. Heritage Quay
3. Red cliff Quay
4. Main Cruise Ships Ports
5. St. John's Cathedral
6. Dickenson Bay beach
7. King Court Tackey (Prince Klass)
8. Antigua Carnival
9. The Museum of Antigua and Barbuda
10. Lebanon Moravian Church
11. Fort James
12. Fort Barrington

St. George
13. Sir Vivian Richards Stadium

St. Peter
14. Parham Town
15. Betty's Hope Plantation

St. Philip
16. Devil's Bridge: Indian Town National Park

St. Mary
17. Jolly Beach
18. Fig Tree Drive

St. Paul
19. St. Barnabas Anglican Church
20. Shirley Heights
21. English Harbour
22. Nelson's Dockyard National Park
23. Falmouth Harbour
24. Fort Berkeley
25. Fort George

Barbuda
26. Frigate Bird Sanctuary

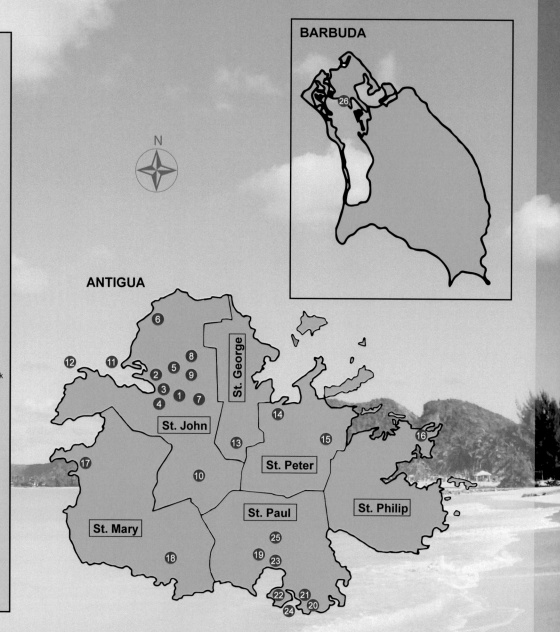

Contents

Preface

All About Antigua and Barbuda was inspired by the natural beauty and history of the twin island nations of Antigua and Barbuda. After many visits and years of reading up on its history, it became pertinent to write a travel book that delves deeper into the history of some of its sites and attractions, with a view to shedding light on aspects of the past that may not be available in similar books.

The book is an informative guide covering key places to visit while in Antigua and Barbuda. It includes over 20 top sites and attractions, including the historically famous Nelson's Dockyard, Betty's Hope, the model sugar plantation that was run by enslaved African labour and St. John's Cathedral, one of the most beautiful historic Cathedrals in the Caribbean. In addition, it contains beautiful colour photographs of each site or attraction and offers an insightful overview of the history, culture and people of Antigua and Barbuda. The photographs featured in this book were taken by the author between the years of 2010 and 2018.

Sincere thanks go to my wife Sheralyn Nathan-Pepple, Dr Radcliffe Robins, John Prince and Valerie Brandes, who all made the time to proof read the book. It is my desire that this book will give the reader a wider perspective of some of Antigua and Barbuda's main sites and attractions.

Michael Nathan-Pepple
Author

Foreword

Michael Nathan-Pepple takes the reader on a personal and intimate tour around Antigua and Barbuda in this beautiful book on its sites and attractions. His guide of the familiar and the not too familiar is a refreshing perspective on the diversity and energy that is Antigua and Barbuda. Each entry is carefully represented as more than just a place to visit – the history and culture of Antigua and Barbuda are brought to life in simple text and pictures.

For an increasing number of visitors, tourism means more than relaxing inside resorts. It's about exploring the country, learning about the culture, interacting with the people and contributing to the development of the destination. The socially conscious tourist will especially enjoy this guide as it juxtaposes the complexity of the Antigua and Barbuda's history with its proud and dynamic present. Whether visiting the Nelson's Dockyard, milling about the busy streets of St. John's or contemplating the twin towers of the Cathedral, the story of Antigua and Barbuda is told as a story of resilience, hope and triumph.

It is my pleasure to commend this guide to you. Antigua and Barbuda will leave a powerful impression on each of your senses. It will be a visit you can never forget.

H.E. Karen-Mae Hill
Antigua and Barbuda,
High Commissioner to the UK

Flag of Antigua and Barbuda

The flag of Antigua and Barbuda was chosen after a flag design competition was launched. The winning design, that of the nationally acclaimed artist and sculptor Sir Reginald Samuel, was officially adopted when Antigua and Barbuda gained "statehood" status (*Self-governing*) on February 27, 1967. The flag is a reflection of the history of the twin island nation of Antigua and Barbuda.

The colours of the flag has distinct meanings. The black is for the African ancestry of the people; blue is for hope and the surrounding sea; red represents the dynamism or energy of the people; white for the numerous sand beaches; the golden yellow image of the sun symbolises the dawning of a new era; and the V-shape is the symbol of victory.

Coat of Arms of Antigua and Barbuda

The coat of arms of Antigua and Barbuda was designed in 1966 by Gordon Christopher, and was officially introduced on 16 February 1967. Although, the coat of arms and flag have similar elements, the symbolism on the coat of arms is slightly more complex.

At the top of the coat of arms is a pineapple, which represents the famous sweet Antigua Black Pineapple. There are several native plants surrounding the shield including red hibiscus, yucca and sugarcane. On either side of the shield is a pair of deer representing the wildlife of the islands.

Inside the shield are elements and colours similar to those on the flag, and a windmill representing the historical sugar cane industry. At the bottom is a scroll containing the national motto: "Each endeavouring, all achieving".

Introduction

The Island of Antigua (*pronounced An-TEE-gah*) was originally inhabited by the Siboney (*'stone age people'*), and later by the Arawaks and the Caribs (*they called themselves 'Kalinago'*). Antigua's indigenous name was Waladli or Wadadli by the local population. Christopher Columbus while on his second voyage to the region in 1493, renamed it Antigua after the Church of Santa Maria de la Antigua in Seville, Spain. In 1632, Antigua was colonised by English settlers from St. Kitts and had its first large sugar estate established in 1674 by Barbadian-born British soldier, plantation and slave-owner Christopher Codrington. Barbuda (*known as Wa'omoni by Caribs*), and sister island to Antigua, was leased by Christopher and John Codrington from the British crown for the nominal price of 'one fat sheep yearly, if demanded.' The Codrington family, originally from Gloucester in the UK, controlled Barbuda from 1685 to 1870 and its only town still bears the founding family's name.

During the second half of the 17th century, thousands of enslaved Africans were imported to work on the numerous sugar plantation estates that were scattered across the Caribbean. They were brought under the most appalling conditions and endured even harsher, inhumane treatments on the plantations. The majority of the enslaved Africans were predominantly from the West African region. However, there were those brought from central Africa (*e.g. the Umbundu*), after the 1730's. In this environment of slavery, Africans were no longer called by their tribes of origin such as Ashanti, Ewe, Yoruba or Igbo and became identified as Negroes or Blacks. After the slaves were emancipated on 1st August 1834, both the Islands of Antigua and Barbuda were administered together as part of the Leeward Islands Federation from 1871-1956.

In 1967, Antigua and Barbuda became a self-governing state within the British Commonwealth and was granted full independence in 1981. However, it remains a constitutional monarchy with the Queen of England, Queen Elizabeth II (*or her successor*) as the head of state. The Queen is represented by a Governor-General who is appointed on the advice of the Prime Minister. Since gaining independence, the economy of Antigua and Barbuda has shifted from agriculture to tourism.

The twin island nation of Antigua and Barbuda comprises the islands of Antigua, Barbuda, Redonda and includes several other smaller islands, namely Long, Green, Great Bird, Guiana, Maiden and York Islands. The capital city of St John's, located in the parish of St John was established as a trading post in 1675 and designed as a city in 1842. It is also home to about a third of the country's population. Today, St John's cosmopolitan atmosphere makes it an excellent hub for shopping and dining.

Antigua and Barbuda is referred to as the "Land of 365 Beaches" because of the numerous white and pink sand beaches that surround the islands. Many of these beaches have beachfront resort hotels that are perfect for weddings, whether in a gazebo by the beach or on the beach itself. Apart from being known for its beautiful beaches, cloudless skies and majestic sunsets, this twin island nation has many historical sites and gorgeous sceneries which are worth visiting.

The majority of Antiguans and Barbudans have African ancestry, however, there is a small segment of the population that are from Europe, America, the Middle East, Asia and other Caribbean islands. Although, the official language is English, the Creole English spoken by most Antiguans and Barbudans is heavily influence by various African languages. All visitors to Antigua and Barbuda can expect to have a great time and a memorable holiday. Welcome to Antigua and Barbuda…Welcome to Paradise!!

BEACH
BAR

JET
BIKES

BEACH
UMBRELLAS

BEACH
CHAIRS

Dickenson Bay Beach

Dickenson Bay beach is a popular destination for both tourists and locals. The bay is lined with a string of large resort hotels such as Sandals Grande Antigua, Antigua Village, Starfish Halcyon Cove Resort and The Siboney Beach Resort. The beachfront boasts numerous restaurants, beach bars, and water sports concessions including kayaks, jet skis, windsurfing, snorkeling and scuba diving. Visitors can cool off in the clear, turquoise warm waters and spend the time drinking cocktails at the various bars along the beach. There are several small uninhabited islands and a one-mile long coral reef just off the coast of the bay. This premier beach is one of the island's 365 beaches and located on the northwestern coast. Other notable beaches worth visiting include Fort James, Long Bay, Pigeon Point, Ffryes Bay, Turner's Beach and Darkwood.

Jolly Beach / Jolly Harbour

Jolly Beach is located within the vicinity of Jolly Harbour. It is a gorgeous one mile white sand beach located in the southwest coast of Antigua. Jolly Beach is home to Starfish Jolly Beach Resort (Formerly Jolly Beach Resort & Spa). The all-inclusive resort overlooks the beach and offers good value accommodation for couples, families and groups.

Jolly Harbour boasts the largest man made marina in the Caribbean. The marina complex was developed on reclaimed swamp land and houses Antigua's first gated community. The luxury villas that make up the community have their own waterfront access and are available for rental.

Jolly Harbour Marina is a full service facility that offers dockage and storage for numerous boats and yachts. Visitors to this safe haven of yacht enthusiasts, can enjoy many amenities including restaurants, bars, car hire, gift shops, banks and a large supermarket. On a clear day, the islands of Montserrat, Nevis and Redonda can be seen from Jolly Beach.

St John's Cruise Ship Port

The main port for cruise ships entering St John's, Antigua is located at Heritage Quay and Redcliff Quay. These cruise docks welcome up to four large ships at any given time and are only a few minutes away from the bustling streets of St. John's. Some of the main cruise lines that have docked in St John's cruise ports, includes Royal Caribbean, Carnival Cruises, Disney and Princess.

Once on the shores of Antigua, cruise-ship passengers can begin to explore the island by walking to some of the capital's top sites such as the Museum of Antigua and Barbuda and the historical St. John's Cathedral, or take taxi and mini-bus guided tours around the island or to one of Antigua's 365 beautiful beaches - one for each day of the year. For those tourists already on the island, cruise ship days can be a good time to visit St. John's, provided you don't mind the crowd and the vibrant atmosphere.

Heritage Quay

Heritage Quay is a modern shopping complex designed to offer duty free shopping to cruise-ship passengers and other tourists on the island. It is the larger of the two Quays in St John's (*the other is Redcliffe Quay*). Heritage Quay offers a wide variety of quality products at very competitive prices such a jewellery, world renowned watches, liquors, designer clothing & footwear, swim wear, perfumes and many other unique souvenir items.

The pedestrian mall within Heritage Quay Complex includes restaurants, bars and a Casino. There is also the vendors' mall located on Thames Street between Heritage and Redcliffe Quays, where visitors can buy even more souvenir items such as tropical clothing, t-shirts, hats and a multitude of locally made art and crafts from local traders. You should be prepared to do a little bartering and enjoy fun shopping.

Historic Redcliffe Quay

Redcliffe Quay offers a unique shopping experience with a wide range of attractive products that you are not likely to find elsewhere. Its various handicraft shops and boutiques, and a small number of bars and restaurants are very popular with visitors. For cruise ship passengers, Redcliffe Quay can be accessed via Heritage Quay by a boardwalk along the south shore of the deep- water harbour. Most of the shops in this historic part of St. John's were converted from old dockside warehouses, some of which date back to the 17th and 18th century.

In Georgian times, Redcliffe Quay was the main trading place in Antigua where goods such as tobacco, rum, cotton and sugar were held. Also contained within this quay, was a compound (*barracoon*) where enslaved Africans were kept until they were sold off to future buyers. The name, Redcliffe, comes from a district of Bristol, England (UK), whose port was a major participant in the Transatlantic Slave Trade. Redcliffe Quay with its colourful colonial era buildings is a place where visitors can buy gifts and souvenirs from locally owned shops and enjoy Caribbean delicacies and refreshments.

Monument to Sir Vere Cornwall Bird

In living memory, Sir Vere Cornwall (V.C) Bird Sr stands supreme as an Antiguan patriot. In his role as a trade union leader, he fought for local workers against oppressive and exploitive working conditions in the sugar industry and sea ports. During the 1960's, he led the move to diversify the economy of Antigua & Barbuda from agriculture to tourism and other service industries. His leadership was responsible for bringing independence to the twin island nation of Antigua and Barbuda, on the 1st of November 1981.

Mr Bird (*or Papa Bird*) is referred to as the Father of the Nation and was the first Prime Minister of Antigua and Barbuda. In 1994, he was made a Knight of the Order of the National Hero by the Government of Antigua and Barbuda. Honourable Vere Cornwall Bird Sr was also awarded the Order of the Caribbean Community by his fellow regional heads of government in 1998, in recognition of his work for regional integration. On the 28th of June 1999, Mr Bird

died at the age of 88. Antigua and Barbuda's international airport is named in his honour. The imposing monument is located near the main Market complex in St John's, a position where the vast majority of those travelling in and out of the city of St. John's must pass.

Prince Klaas Monument

During the many bitter years of African enslavement in Antigua (*from the 16th to the 19th centuries*), King Court Tackey, popularly known as Prince Klaas stands unchallenged as an Antiguan hero. Prince Klaas was an enslaved African who is credited with organising a rebellion on the island of Antigua in 1736. Born in Ghana (*formerly the Gold Coast*) in 1691, he was brought to Antigua at the age of 10 years old. During his years as a slave, Klaas refused to let go of his Africanness and yearned for him and his people to be free.

In a ritual declaration of war on the slave owners, Prince Klass was crowned 'King of the Coromantees' in a secret oath ceremony. Unfortunately, his plot was discovered and he was horrifically executed, alongside his chief ringleaders, Tomboy and Hercules in October 1736. In total, 88 slaves were burned or tortured to death. The exact location of these executions is unknown, however, some evidence places the site at the Antiguan Recreation Ground.

The monument of King Court Tackey (Prince Klass) is located on Independence Drive in St. John's. It stands as a memorial dedicated to the leader of a rebellion in Antigua. The monument is also a reminder of the cruelty and inhumanity of slavery, in Antigua and many other Caribbean islands. Prince Klaas is one of Antigua and Barbuda's national heroes and his life together with others like him, is celebrated on the country's National Heroes' Day. This memorable day gives the people of Antigua and Barbuda the opportunity to commemorate the lives of those who have made significant contributions to the country.

Museum of Antigua and Barbuda

The Museum of Antigua and Barbuda was founded in 1985 and housed in the old court house, which was built in 1750. The building is one of the most historic buildings still in use in St. John's and was built of yellow free stone quarried from a number of Antigua's surrounding islands. The museum was set up with the main purpose of telling the story of this twin island nation. The exhibits on display span a wide range covering geographical, historical, cultural artefacts, which collectively give a very clear picture of the country's past and its development. Incidentally, the old court house was built on the site of the first Sunday Market for the enslaved Africans, who came from all over Antigua to sell their produce.

The museum showcases the history of the island's creation, its original inhabitants, its naval history, the slavery experience which dominated the economy and societal development of the islands for centuries. Also on display, is a statue of Sir Isaac Vivian Alexander Richards (the world renowned cricketer and living sporting National Hero of Antigua and Barbuda). In addition, the museum has a reference library that is open to the public. Although the museum is small in size, it is however, loaded with historical information and artefacts that will give visitors a good background history of Antigua and Barbuda. The museum is located at the corner of Long and Market Streets. A visit is highly recommended and the entry fee is reasonable. The museum is an invaluable educational resource for research students at any level both local and international.

15

PAUL

HUDSON-HUNSLET

BETTY'S HOPE LOCOMOTIVE DISPLAY

A total of twenty six narrow gauge locomotives were imported into Antigua between 1904 and 1948
to provide motive power for the island's sugar cane railways.
Twenty one for the Antigua Sugar Factory at Gunthorpes and five for Bendals Sugar Factory.

The four locomotives on display have been refurbished
by Lowveanos Gameson (UK)
with the assistance of
The Ministry of Tourism,
The Ministry of Public Works
& The Museum of Antigua and Barbuda
in order to preserve a piece of
Antigua's by-gone history.

Betty's Hope Plantation

Betty's Hope was a sugarcane plantation established on the eastern part of Antigua. The plantation was founded in 1651 by Christopher Keynell, governor of Antigua between 1653 and 1660. In 1674, Christopher Codrington, Governor of the Leeward Islands, acquired the estate and named it Betty's Hope, after his daughter. Under the ownership of the Codrington's, the plantation was transformed into a large-scale sugar estate and flourished as an agricultural industrial enterprise. Betty's Hope was the largest and most productive of over 190 sugar plantations that dotted the islands landscape during the centuries of slavery. Like every other sugar plantation in the Caribbean, it relied heavily on enslavement for labour.

In its 300 year history, Betty's Hope played a key role in the history of Antigua and Barbuda and had a tremendous impact on the lives of many generations of Antiguans. The Codrington Family's ownership of Betty's Hope ended in 1944, when it was sold to the Antigua Syndicate Estates Ltd. A visit to Betty's Hope is a chance to see a restored working mill and experience a tangible insight into the past. Although most of the buildings are in ruins, plaques have been placed where key buildings once stood such as the Great House and the enslaved quarters. The estate's former cotton house storeroom has been

converted into a visitor's centre and museum. The latter gives visitors an opportunity to learn about the plantation's history and the extreme hardship the enslaved had to endure. Betty's Hope is a popular tourist site and a must-see for history students and people interested in historical sites.

Devil's Bridge:
Indian Town National Park

Devil's bridge is a natural limestone rock arch, or bridge that was formed over thousands of years by seawater erosion. It is a truly spectacular sight and located on the most easterly point on the island. The waves are particularly fierce due to the lack of land between this part of the coast and the continent of Africa. The bridge and the surrounding area forms part of the Indian Town National Park.

Devil's bridge is said to have gained its name from the tragic events that took place during the days of enslavement. It is detailed in a famous Antiguan book "To Shoot Hard Labour" that many of the enslaved from neighbouring plantations would go to this spot and throw themselves into the sea rather than submit to enslavement.

Since the spot was an area of mass suicide, local people concluded that the devil must be present there. A visit to Devil's Bridge is an opportunity to discover the power of nature and get some great photos of the waves from the Atlantic Ocean splashing up against the bridge and surrounding rocks.

31

English Harbour

English Harbour the most strategic and military naval base for British vessels in the Caribbean, is a naturally sheltered deep-water harbour located in the south eastern-coast of Antigua. It is the heart of British colonial history in the Caribbean and was first used for careening and re-fitting of warships in the 1650's. For 300 years, the harbour was home to the British Navy and used strategically to position and protect ships and cargo from devastating hurricanes, marauding pirates and for monitoring French naval activities.

English Harbour is best known for housing Nelson's Dockyard, a former British Naval base and contains most of the island's top sites. It is today acknowledged as the sailing hub of the Caribbean and host many world renowned regattas, including the Classic Yacht Regatta and Antigua Sailing Week. This famous and historical harbour is the name given to Antigua's premium rum, English Harbour Rum, which can be purchased from any duty free shop on the island.

Nelson's Dockyard National Park

Nelson's Dockyard (*originally 'His Majesty's Antigua Naval Yard'*) is a historical site located within the confines of Antigua's largest National Park. Construction of the dockyard began at English Harbour in 1725 and was made possible with the labour of generations of enslaved Africans. According to Hewlester Samuel's book 'The birth of the village of Liberta', reference was made to the fact that 'where Nelson's Dockyard is located was a fifty-foot hill; it took one hundred and fifty slaves to level the hill so the fort could be built.' The dockyard was used by the British Navy to carry out repairs on British warships, throughout the Eastern Caribbean.

On 14th November 1961, the renovated former British Naval dockyard was opened as a heritage tourism site and named after Admiral Horatio Nelson, who was stationed in Antigua from 1784-87.

Many of the dockyard's old colonial buildings have been restored and turned into restaurants, hotels, gift shops and other businesses. The dockyard's museum is situated in the Naval Officer's House and presents the history of Nelson's Dockyard alongside exhibits that showcases current archaeological and historical research in Antigua. Nelson's Dockyard is the only working Georgian-era dockyard in the world and is the biggest tourist attraction on the island. In 2016, it was made a UNESCO World Heritage site. Admission ticket to the Nelson's Dockyard, can also be used for entry to the Dow's Hill Interpretation Centre, where visitors can enjoy lovely views and watch a short video presentation about the history, culture and heritage of Antigua and Barbuda.

Falmouth Harbour

Falmouth Harbour is a horseshoe-shaped bay and natural harbour which is located on the southern coast of Antigua, immediately west of English Harbour. Within the northern shore of the harbour, the English established the first major settlement on the island in 1632. The harbour, once a safe place to anchor ships during hurricanes, is still in use today and houses a full service marina which was purposely built to cater for larger yachts. There are also a wide variety of restaurants, bars, boutiques, recreational attractions and the lovely Pigeon Point beach. From this popular family-friendly beach, visitors can go on a hike over the hill to the historic and very picturesque English Harbour. Falmouth Harbour is also home to the Antigua Yacht Club Marina Resort, which offers guests the opportunity to enjoy Antiguan hospitality.

Shirley Heights

Shirley Heights is a military fort named after Sir Thomas Shirley, who served as the Governor of the Leeward Islands in 1781. It was built overlooking the Caribbean Sea and used as a lookout for incoming ships. Shirley Heights is a great spot to walk, take fabulous photos, see spectacular sunsets and experience the best views on the island. The fort comprises of Dow's Hill, The Ridge and Artillery Quarters, Blockhouse and The Lookout.

The Lookout is a high point (*about 490 ft.*) that affords a superb view of English and Falmouth Harbours. The scene is often used as the iconic image of Antigua. This venue is used to host the famous Shirley Heights late Sunday afternoon 'party' from 4pm until 10pm. The 'must attend-party' is an opportunity to meet people from all over the world, as well as locals. Revellers are treated to the sound of steel bands and tasty spicy barbeque food. So, if you're planning a trip to Antigua, this has to be on your list of things to do.

Antigua Forts

Antigua was popularly referred to as one of Britain's crown jewels in the Caribbean. Evidence of this can be seen in many of the historical military fortifications established around the coast of Antigua. Between the 17th century and later part of the 19th century, Antigua is said to have been one of the most heavily fortified places in the world. Although most of these forts have fallen into ruins, they still provide some insight into Antigua's colonial past and the great effort made by Antiguan plantation owners and the British government to protect it from foreign invasions. The strategic positions of these forts make them good destinations to explore and get some of the best views on the island.

Fort James is situated at the entrance of St. John's (*north side of St John's Harbour*) and built to protect St. John's Harbour. Construction of the fort started in 1706, however, most of the buildings were built in 1739. The fort is named after King James II of England and is the only fort to still have all its original ten great guns intact. A visit to Fort James gives visitors a superb view of the harbour and access to many bars and restaurants within its vicinity. Also nearby is Fort James beach, one of the most beautiful beaches in Antigua.

Fort Barrington is located at the top of Goat Hill (*south side of St. John's Harbour*) in Five Islands. Just like Fort James, it was built to protect St John's Harbour and also used as a lookout station to report the movement of ships. The first fort sited on this hill was built in the 1650s, while the present fortification was constructed in 1779. Fort Barrington was named after Admiral Barrington (1729-1800) and remains

Fort James

the only fort in Antigua to have experienced military action. Its vantage hilltop position, allow visitors to enjoy the stunning views of the Caribbean Sea.

Fort Berkeley was built in stages between 1704 and 1745, with the sole purpose of defending English Harbour, particularly the Dockyard. It is situated on the western entrance to English Harbour and had 29 large cannons positioned to repel any potential assault. The harbour was never attacked and the presence of the cannons seem to have acted as a deterrent. The views from Fort Berkeley are incredible and the site is one of the most popular places for tourists to take photographs. The fort is only accessible by foot and takes between 15-20 minutes to walk from Nelson's Dockyard.

Fort George is the largest fortification on Antigua (*over eight acres in size*) and located on the summit of Monk's Hill. It was named Great George Fort after the Patron Saint of England and built to guard Falmouth Bay. The fort was to serve as a place of refuge for the women and children of the inhabitants of Antigua, in the event of either a slave insurrection or invasion by the Caribs and other European powers. Like other forts on the island, its construction relied heavily on using enslaved labour. During the sixteen years (*1689-1715*) that it took to build the fort, hundreds of enslaved men were pulled off the plantations and worked for six days a week, for up to six months at a time. The choice to erect the fort at the top of Monks Hill was due to its commanding views of Falmouth and the surrounding areas. Among the ruins are the sites for 32 cannons, water cisterns and some of the original buildings.

Fort Berkeley

St. John's Cathedral

St. John's Cathedral, also known as the St. John the Divine, is an Anglican church perched on a hilltop in St. John's. It is the most prominent landmark in St John's and the Cathedral Church of the Diocese of North Eastern Caribbean and Aruba. The present church with its imposing twin towers was built in 1845 but opened for public worship in 1847 and consecrated as a Cathedral in 1848.

There were two previous churches with the same name that were built within the compound of the present Cathedral and Churchyard. The first church was a wooden building constructed in 1681, while the second church was built in 1746. These churches were subsequently destroyed by earthquakes in 1745 and 1843 respectively. According to the memoirs of Samuel Smith (*To Shoot Hard Labour*), "the planter class called the Cathedral 'Big Church' and that it frightened the people as a symbol of English power." He also indicated that the black population who were previously excluded from being part of the Anglican Church, only started getting more involved at about the time of the First World War. After many years of restoration work, worship services are once more being held at this historical church.

St. Barnabas Anglican Church

St. Barnabas Anglican Church in Liberta was built as a chapel school in the 1670s. After the destruction of the mother church in Falmouth (*St Paul's*), as a result of the 1843 earthquake, St Barnabas became the primary place of worship for the Anglican congregation across the Parish of Saint Paul. The unique church is constructed with red brick and locally sourced green limestone. The limestone is exclusive to the southern districts of Antigua.

St Barnabas is a church with lots of history and was devoted to the apostle Saint Barnabas, one of the earliest seafaring saints. This charming little church sits on Barnabas Hill and can be seen when passing through the village of Liberta en route to English Harbour. A quick stop over is highly recommended.

43

Lebanon Moravian Church / Sea View Farm

The Lebanon Moravian Church in Sea View Farm village is one of the many historical churches dotted across the island nation of Antigua and Barbuda. The Church started as a mission on the 19th of May 1838. In 1840, a female teachers' training school opened in Lebanon and provided education to train women to be teachers. The school was later moved to Spring Gardens in 1854 and was one of the earliest educational institutions in the Caribbean.

The village of Sea View Farm was one of the many villages established after emancipation. It is the home of pottery in Antigua and famous for its traditional handmade clay pots, which dates back to a period when enslaved Africans moulded cooking pots from local clay. In fact, archaeological evidence places Antigua's earliest 'Afro-Caribbean' made pottery in the early 1700s. Whilst pottery making once played a significant role in Antigua and Barbuda's economy, this local industry has declined over the years and today mainly produce for the tourist market. If you are interested in products made out of clay such as flowerpots, miniature coal pots, candle lamps and other items, you can stop by at Elvie's Pottery in Sea View Farm and experience pottery making using indigenous African techniques.

Fig Tree Drive

Many would say Antigua isn't Antigua if you don't get to travel to Fig Tree Drive. This part of the Island is very lush and green, and its landscape is dotted with banana trees (*called 'figs' locally*) and an abundance of tropical fruit trees such as guavas, mangoes, oranges and coconuts. The 5-mile-long drive is like going through a tropical wonderland, with fantastic views and breathtaking sights.

Along the way you will pass small villages such as Swetes and John Hughes, the zip line centre and road side traders selling bananas and the famous Antiguan black pineapple. This pineapple is claimed to be the best in the world, mainly for its texture and sweetness. The road also leads to the beautiful beaches in the south such as Darkwood and Valley Church. The whole experience of driving down Fig Tree Drive provides an intimate glimpse of Antigua. The drive should be a 'must do' on your itinerary while in Antigua but remember to keep your eyes on the road.

Antigua Carnival

The Antiguan Carnival is a celebration of the emancipation of slavery and held annually from the end of July to the first Tuesday in August. The genesis of the festival dates back to 1st August 1834, when slavery was abolished. History records that the people went on the street and celebrated their joy and happiness to be free. This carnival like atmosphere began to be celebrated at Christmas and subsequently, evolved into the Antiguan Carnival in 1957.

Today's carnival showcases a number of events including the Party Monarch and Calypso Monarch competitions, the Panorama steel band competition and the spectacular Parade of Bands. Revellers can also attend local concerts, food fairs and cultural shows. The finale of the carnival is the first Monday and Tuesday in August, which are public holidays. Both days see the highlight of 'mas' (*short for masquerade*), as troupes with extravagant costumes accompanied by beautifully decorated floats, parade on the streets of St. John's. Carnival season is the perfect time to come and experience the culture, music and uniqueness of the people of Antigua and Barbuda.

Sir Vivian Richards Stadium

Sir Vivian Richards Stadium is located in the North Sound area of Antigua. The stadium was built to host the 2007 Cricket World Cup and is named after the nation's favourite sporting hero, and former West Indies cricket captain, Sir Isaac Vivian Alexander Richards, known as Vivian (Viv) Richards. The Antiguan sports legend popularly known during his career days as the 'Master Blaster' led a West Indian team that dominated the cricket world during the 1970s and 80s. However, it was at the Antigua Recreation Grounds, in St John's, that Sir Viv and the West Indies cricket team made some of the most memorable cricketing history.

Sir Vivian Richards Stadium has a holding capacity of approximately 10,000 spectators and is easily accessible from the airport. Some cricket fans are of the opinion that the stadium is a great place to watch cricket, especially with a good crowd. Sir Viv's statue is proudly displayed outside this ultra-modern cricket ground.

Parham Town

Parham is a small historical town located in the north-east of Antigua. It was established as Antigua's first capital and port in 1663, and became the centre of sea trade. Parham got its name from the title of Lord William Willoughby of Parham. The title 'Parham' has its origin in Suffolk, England. Like other parts of Antigua at the time, the cultivation of sugarcane was the order of the day and the largest sugar plantation in Parham was owned by the Tudway family from 1679-1944. The surviving records of the family's ownership of the plantation (*known as the Tudway papers*), provides an insight into the operations of a typical sugar plantation in Antigua and the wider Caribbean region.

This sleepy town of just under 1300 people, offers attractions worth exploring including, Great Bird Island and St. Peter's Anglican Church. The Anglican Church with its irregular octagonal shape and unusual wooden roof was built in 1840. It remains one of the important landmarks on the island of Antigua.

Parham is on the shore of Parham Harbour, a well-protected anchorage, which was busy for two centuries until the decline of sugar exports in 1920. Today, the harbour is equipped with a fisheries complex, where fishermen bring, store and sell their daily catch. In 2013, the people of Parham celebrated 363 years of history.

Barbuda

Barbuda is Antigua's sister island and located approximately 30 miles north of Antigua. It is 62 square miles in area and rises to 128 feet in an area known as the highlands. The Amerindian called this exotic Caribbean island "Wa'omoni", meaning land of herons. This island that boasts some of the best beaches in the world was once the private estate of the Codrington family. It was leased from the British crown and used to provide supplies such as ground provisions, fish, livestock, timber and slaves for sugar plantations owned by the Codringtons in Antigua and Barbados. The reason why sugar was not cultivated in Barbuda was because of its arid land, which could not sustain large scale sugar production.

One of the major attractions of Barbuda is the Frigate Bird Sanctuary, which is located in the Codrington Lagoon National Park. The frigate bird colony on Barbuda is one of the largest in the world. Barbuda's magnificent stretches of pristine pink and white sand beaches are great for fishing, diving and snorkeling. As a result of the island's limestone composition, Barbuda has a few caves to explore on the Atlantic side of the Island. In September 2017, Barbuda was struck by Hurricane Irma which destroyed a large part of its infrastructure. This paradise island which is full of resilient people, is working to revive its lobster and fishing industry and is making its way back to becoming a popular tourist destination again.

Visitors wanting to travel to Barbuda from Antigua can either go by air or sea. The Barbuda Express ferry service offers daily trips between Antigua and Barbuda (*weather permitting*), which leaves from St. John's port and takes about 90 minutes.

Other sites and attractions worth visiting

Antigua

- Dow's Hill Interpretation Centre
- Clarence House
- Mount Obama (*formerly Boggy Peak*)
- Antigua's Donkey Sanctuary
- Stingray City
- Rainforest Zipline Tours
- Harmony Hall
- Pillars of Hercules
- Wadadli Animal Nature Park
- Megaliths of Greencastle Hill
- Antigua Sailing Week (*usually commences end of April*)

Barbuda

- Various beautiful beaches (*including 17-Mile Beach*)
- Martello Tower
- Darby's Cave
- The Caves at Two Foot Bay

Some useful information while in Antigua and Barbuda

Electric Voltage - 110 and 220 volts can be found on the island. Most hotels have both voltages available.

Shopping Hours - Monday to Saturday 9:00am to 5:00pm. Although many stores still close at noon on Thursdays.

Currency - The Eastern Caribbean Dollar (EC$) is the official currency of Antigua and Barbuda. It is fixed to the US dollar at around US$1=EC$2.7. US dollars and major credit cards are widely accepted.

Banks - opening and closing times are Monday to Thursday from 8:00 am to 2:00 pm, and Friday from 8:00am to 4:00pm.

Weather & Climate - Antigua and Barbuda is warm throughout the year and daytime temperatures are usually between 24 and 30 degrees. The temperatures at night varies from 20 to 27 degrees. A cool breeze is guaranteed all year round.

Duty Free Shopping is available to visitors, in St. John's within the Heritage Quay Shopping centre, Redcliffe Quay and at the airport. To be eligible to buy duty free goods, you must show a valid airline ticket and some form of identification (e.g. passport).

Car rental - affordable rates are on offer for different types of vehicles. On production of a valid driver's license, you can obtain a temporary 90 day driving license for EC$50 (US$20).

Driving is on the left hand side of the road and most cars are right hand drive. Speed limits are posted in miles.

Emergency Numbers/Contacts - 999 and 911 are the general numbers emergency numbers to call while in Antigua and Barbuda.

The International Direct Dialling (IDD) Code for Antigua and Barbuda is +1 268, which is followed by a seven digit island number.

Personal Safety - The islands of Antigua & Barbuda are relatively safe. However, it is important to take practical precautions; i.e. note emergency numbers, always lock your room/house/vehicle; don't wear expensive jewellery, and secure all valuables and travel documents.